D1716422

GRAVITY

by Meg Gaertner

Cody Koala

An Imprint of Pop!
popbooksonline.com

abdobooks.com

Published by Pop!, a division of ABDO, PO Box 398166, Minneapolis, Minnesota 55439. Copyright © 2020 by POP, LLC. International copyrights reserved in all countries. No part of this book may be reproduced in any form without written permission from the publisher. Pop!™ is a trademark and logo of POP, LLC.

Printed in the United States of America, North Mankato, Minnesota

052019
092019

THIS BOOK CONTAINS
RECYCLED MATERIALS

Cover Photo: iStockphoto
Interior Photos: iStockphoto, 1, 5 (top), 7, 8, 11, 14–15, 17 (feather), 17 (brick), 20–21; Shutterstock Images, 5 (bottom left), 5 (bottom right), 13, 19

Editor: Connor Stratton
Series Designer: Sarah Taplin

Library of Congress Control Number: 2018964774
Publisher's Cataloging-in-Publication Data
Names: Gaertner, Meg, author.
Title: Gravity / by Meg Gaertner.
Description: Minneapolis, Minnesota : Pop!, 2020 | Series: Science all around | Includes online resources and index.
Identifiers: ISBN 9781532163579 (lib. bdg.) | ISBN 9781532165016 (ebook)
Subjects: LCSH: Gravity--Juvenile literature. | Weight--Juvenile literature. | Gravitation--Juvenile literature. | Science--Juvenile literature.
Classification: DDC 531.14--dc23

Hello! My name is

Cody Koala

Pop open this book and you'll find QR codes like this one, loaded with information, so you can learn even more!

Scan this code* and others like it while you read, or visit the website below to make this book pop.

popbooksonline.com/gravity

*Scanning QR codes requires a web-enabled smart device with a QR code reader app and a camera.

Table of Contents

What Is Gravity?

A girl throws a ball.

The ball always comes back

down. The girl jumps up.

She always comes back to

the ground. This downward

force is called **gravity**.

Watch a video here!

Matter

Gravity pulls **matter** together. Matter is what makes up everything that exists. Matter takes up space. Matter also has **mass**.

Learn more here!

Mass is the amount
of matter in an object.
Gravity is the pull between
two masses. Gravity causes
two objects with mass
to move toward each other.

The earth and moon are both
objects with mass. Earth's gravity
pulls the moon around it.

Gravity's pull depends on the mass of objects. Objects with large masses have a strong pull. Objects with small masses have a weaker pull.

Gravity's pull also depends on distance. Objects closer together feel a stronger pull.

Chapter 3

Falling Objects

Earth's **mass** is huge. It has a strong **force** of **gravity**. Earth pulls **matter** toward it. This is why things fall down.

Complete an activity here!

Gravity makes things gain
speed as they fall. On Earth,
air pushes back against
falling objects.

This force is called **air resistance**. It makes objects fall more slowly.

A vacuum is a space with no air. In a vacuum, only gravity affects how fast an object falls. If you drop a feather and a brick, they will fall at the same speed.

On Earth, air resistance affects some objects more than others. A feather will fall more slowly than a brick.

In a vacuum, there is no air. A feather and a brick will fall at the same speed.

Chapter 4

Weight and Gravity

Weight measures **gravity's** effect on an object. For example, a rock has a certain weight on Earth. But it would have a different weight on the moon.

Learn more here!

The moon's **mass** is smaller than Earth's. That means the effect of gravity is smaller too. Objects weigh less on the moon than they do on Earth.

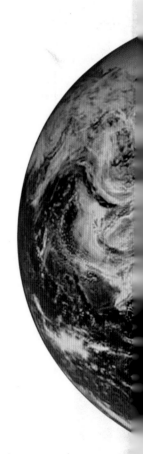

Making Connections

Text-to-Self

When have you seen gravity at work?
Give three examples.

Text-to-Text

Have you read other books about gravity, matter, or mass? What did you learn?

Text-to-World

Name three things in your home or school that have large masses. Can you think of three other things with small masses?

Glossary

air resistance – the force of air that pushes back against a moving object.

force – something that changes the movement of an object.

gravity – a force that pulls together any objects with mass.

mass – a measure of the amount of matter in an object.

matter – anything with mass that takes up space.

weight – a measure of how strongly gravity pulls on an object.

Index

Online Resources

popbooksonline.com

Thanks for reading this Cody Koala book!

Scan this code* and others like it in this book, or visit the website below to make this book pop!

popbooksonline.com/gravity

*Scanning QR codes requires a web-enabled smart device with a QR code reader app and a camera.